WOMANKRAFT COMMUNITY ARTS

50 YEARS OF PRESENTING WOMEN'S VISION

JUDY JENNINGS

With N. Skreko Martin

WomanKraft Community Arts

Front Cover Photo Credit Nicole Young

ISBN: 9798329376647

This book is dedicated to the forward thinking dreamers; the poets, painters, sculptors and singers, the ones who have continuously said "yes" to art;

To the countless number of hardworking volunteers who've supported WomanKraft over the years, doing whatever needed to be done, literally keeping the doors open;

To the donors who have helped to make WomanKraft the success it is today, we couldn't have done it without you;

To the founding mothers who set it all in motion;

You are the ones who've breathed life into WomanKraft for the past 50 years.

THE WOMANKRAFT MOSIAC

WomanKraft Community Arts is the story of a dedicated group of women artists in Tucson who banded together in the 1970s in response to the lack of female gallery representation in the fine arts world. More than just an account of community based art; these pages tell of the determination of the founding mothers who collectively built a space for art, lost it all, and rebuilt.

These chapters are a collection of stories about artists looking for community, and finding the talent within themselves. Some of them consist of an artist's own words as told to me, as in chapter one, "Art in Alternative Spaces; Nancy Speaks". Other sections are written by me.

These stories are the tiles of the mosaic of Womankraft. This book is a celebration of the resilient spirit of the long-lived community arts group; giving space to the vision of women and other underrepresented artists for 50 years, and still counting!

Judy Jennings

Alison Hughes served as president of the Tucson Chapter, National Organization for Women, and was the first executive director of the Tucson Women's Commission during the founding years of these organizations. She has been a community activist throughout her life.

In the early 60's I enrolled in a sculpture class at Corcoran Gallery of Art. The classroom was located in the gallery basement. On a wall at the bottom of the stairs my eyes were drawn to a large, wooden, black sculpture mounted on the wall next to the classroom door. It was a sculpture by Louise Nevelson. I frequently stopped to gaze in wonderment at this Nevelson piece and questioned why it was in the old basement and not upstairs in the gallery. Women authors faced similar barriers like those experienced by Nevelson and women of color were under-represented in the arts. Such was the fate of women's art. But something new was happening.

The feminist movement of the 60's and 70's was growing in response to years of misogyny. The first chapters of the National Organization for Women and the National Women's Political Caucus were organized. Government commissions on women were established at national, state and local levels including the Tucson Women's Commission. The Black Women's Task Force of Tucson grew out of the Tucson Women's Commission and remains a vibrant, active organization today. The Equal Rights Amendment was once again introduced in Congress and sent to the states for ratification. In spite of marches and sit-ins by thousands of women throughout the country the amendment has not yet become law.

In Tucson, women artists and writers took matters into their own hands. They formed WomanKraft and told their own stories publicly in beautiful poetry, essays, plays, paintings, and sculptures. These artists were, and remain, truth-tellers who have helped to re-shape their story. Their story is Our story. It foretells our vision of a future in which the talents of women in the arts are genuinely appreciated. "WomanKraft Community Arts" offers a historical breakthrough into the lives of Tucson's talent. It is an honor to have known most of the women featured in this book.

Alison Hughes

TABLE OF CONTENTS

CHAPTER 1

ART IN ALTERNATIVE SPACES, NANCY SPEAKS

Nancy Martin, known professionally as N. Skreko Martin, one of six Founding Mothers

Contributing Artist since 1974

Secretary WomanKraft Board of Directors and Chief Grant Writer since 1997

Website: artfactswest.com

N. Skreko Martin sorting pipe in her studio yard.

"In 1974, things were very different.

I'll tell you my own story, which I think is typical of women in the arts at that time. I took my Bachelors degree in 1960 and completed my Master's in '68. During that time I found that if I submitted my slides as Nancy Martin, I got rejected more often than I expected and my work was considered 'crude'. But when I finally decided to go with the androgynous N. Skreko Martin, and was probably presumed to be male, suddenly my work became 'strong'.

A lot of women artists were having the same problem. We were into the second wave of feminism and a group of us came together here in Tucson. There was also a group in Phoenix and a statewide Arizona Women's Caucus For The Arts.

Originally, this small group of founders had the idea to rent a space and have our own gallery, so we incorporated as a non-profit. Then we found that actually getting a space and figuring out how to have it open and somebody there was a bit more than we could manage.

At that point we were offered locations to show our work, and one of the first to do that was Cele Peterson, who had dress shops, and she offered us a wall on the second floor in her downtown store on Pennington. Is this anything anybody even remembers anymore? That was our first show.

Susan Chambers in WomanKraft Booth, Tucson Museum of Art Craft Fair, 1975

We used to collectively show at the Tucson Museum of Art Spring and Fall craft shows, and at St. Phillips in the Hills Episcopal Church Spring Arts Festival. WomanKraft had a group show at the University of Arizona student union in 1975, and we took part in organizing the statewide show *Women/Arizona'75* along with The Circle from Phoenix. In '77 we organized an exhibit that was shown in the gallery at Pima College and created the *WomanKraft at Pima 1977* catalog.

We were pretty much holding meetings at somebody's kitchen table and showing in alternative spaces, and we did that for a long time. Then we noticed that performance artists (who are better than visual artists at getting grants, since they're out in the public eye, while visual artists tend to be isolated in their studios) were getting funding through a manpower training act called CETA.

In 1979 WomanKraft, the Southern Arizona Clay and Glass Cooperative, and a consortium of other arts and crafts groups put together a proposal (which I pretty much wrote) and we got a grant-in 1979! -for $74,000. Schools wanted us to come and speak at career days, give presentations, and talk to classes about being an artist. Of course many artists were, then and now, low income people who were the least able to do volunteer time like that. Sometimes they'd buy you lunch. So we said we'd put artists out into the community. We held classes at the Jewish Community Center, the School for the Deaf and Blind, Tucson House, Prince of Tucson trailer park and other senior centers. We had the classes available for when they were wanted.

The artists were paid minimum wage for classroom time, and also for studio and meeting time. We eventually got yearly funding of over $90,000 until 1984. Unfortunately, Jimmy Carter was not reelected and Reagan did not approve of funding the arts, so that was the end of CETA. WomanKraft began seeking alternative funding sources from the Arizona Commission on the Arts, and the Tucson/Pima Commission on the Arts.

Joy Holdread and Darwin Hall Painting Crime Prevention Mural at the Tucson Convention Center. Community Artists Project/CETA, 1980.

About that time Carol Kestler, another founding mother, decided she wanted to launch a program to make art instruction available in underserved schools. WomanKraft gave her our blessing and a small allowance toward incorporation, and she spun off to start Arts Genesis, where she was executive director until she passed in 2015.

After CETA ended, I stepped away to take a position as an art gallery director and Linn Lane took over as WomanKraft Executive Director. Linn had always wanted a facility and after she assumed that role, that's when WomanKraft opened the gallery on Congress Street.

Downtown Tucson in the 1970's was a wasteland. Of course artists, who are always sort of courageous about these things, went into deserted storefronts they could rent for chump change, and they had studios down there. I remember otherwise it was pretty much just dive bars back then.

Eventually in the mid-1980s, artisan galleries started opening up downtown and WomanKraft was one of the first. Dinnerware Gallery and the Central Art Collective gallery were there, now long gone and forgotten. The Screening Room was also there and they're still around. WomanKraft went into a vacated optician's office owned by the Carroll family on the corner of Sixth Street and Congress Avenue. Gladys Carroll liked WomanKraft and she used to have Linn Lane over to her home for tea and cookies. The building was a disaster, so in exchange for nominal rent, WomanKraft invested thousands of hours of sweat equity fixing it up, including installing two bathrooms.

Unfortunately, when Gladys Carroll died, the 'liberal arts supporting' side of her family wanted to keep the family home, so the 'Family Life Radio' part got the commercial properties. They took one look at our art and immediately raised the rent to an impossible amount. We had done all of this rehab on their property and we were out the door. That was when WomanKraft bought the Castle, which was also a condemned property, but at least we knew the sweat equity we would put into it would be ours.

That's pretty much the litany of artists going into areas; it's happened in New York, in Chicago, in San Francisco. Then artists started getting smart about equity, and WomanKraft kind of wrote the book on that in Tucson.

One of the things we've continued to do right over the years is that we empower the workers. How many nonprofits have a board that dictates to the volunteers? But at WomanKraft it's the volunteers who run things. That's what I call the WomanKraft Empowerment Model. Our incorporation papers and bylaws are such that bureaucracy is minimalized. We set it so that those present at a board meeting constitute a quorum, so we don't have the problem a lot of nonprofits have when not enough people show up to get anything done.

I'm not sure there isn't an element of luck involved, too. The Great Goddess watching out for her women. It seems every time a key person has had a meltdown, there's been somebody else willing to step up. That's been really important, because we've seen so many other nonprofits die out when there was nobody to take over.

We were always doing grant writing and we have a very good record until currently, when I'm the only grant writer left, and I'm fading fast. Come on, I'm past my sell by date! I don't even take two year subscriptions to magazines anymore. It's not that I'm feeling bad, but I'm 85 this year and nobody on either side of my family has ever made it that long. I am definitely feeling the need to train my replacements in the world. Remember how the first thing you do when you take a new job is train your replacement? That's become increasingly difficult.

I do think things have improved in the arts world since the 1970s. Gallery owners have started looking more favorably at women artists and adding them to their stables. Even the big collections like the New York Metropolitan and the Smithsonian are showing more women, and flexing about what they consider to be 'art' to include what used to be called 'craft'. For example, ceramic sculpture and fiber art sculptures are now being recognized as 'sculpture', when they were 'decorative arts' before.

WomanKraft as always been gay friendly. We've shown some blatantly lesbian art which nobody else ever would have shown, and a lot of outsider art, which includes anime and naive art.

Just recently, as I closed my studio and downsized to a casita, I decided to offer some of the artists works I had, which was some nice blue-chip stuff, to the Tucson Museum of Art. And the curator, Julie Sasse, took only the women's work! She said 'We're trying to balance our collection.'

Then Wyatt Anthony, a wonderful photographer who had been associated with WomanKraft for a long time, died and her family was only interested in the family photographs. They didn't understand her art *at all*. It was the usual story; she was the lesbian in the fundamentalist Christian family. So I collected it because I didn't want to see it to go into the dumpster, and I took it to the Arizona Historical Society and they accepted her entire archive! They said 'Oh yes, we're trying to *balance our collection!* We've got too much Wyatt Earp and Doc Holliday. We're lacking in women's vision.'

Wow! That I should have lived so long! Can you believe it?"

CHAPTER 2

CARETAKERS OF CULTURE, 1974-1980

"to be an artist is to be the caretaker of culture,

to reclaim what was to be wasted.

to grow life from the seed of emotion,

to make beauty where there was none,

to open the doors for others to enter,

the home made is the wild heart of our humanness,

we call art"

From "Tribute to Working Women Artists" by Linn Lane

The feminist movement may have erupted during the 1970s but the majority of art gallery owners, who were for the most part wealthy white men, still held the assumption that women don't make fine arts, they make crafts. In those days even photography wasn't considered to be fine art.

There were six women artists in Tucson who had gotten pretty tired of that, so they decided to take matters into their own hands and incorporate as a nonprofit arts organization. They were Amy Ackerman, Janet Burner, Susan Chambers, Doña DiConcini, Carol Kestler, and Nancy Martin. They chose the name WomanKraft because Kraft with a capital K means "power" in German, and it stood for "claiming, validating and empowering the cultural contributions of women". Incorporation took place on the 6th day of August, 1974.

Playwright and poet Linn Lane watched the development of WomanKraft with interest, but since she wasn't a visual artist she wasn't part of the startup group. Before long they expanded to include all of the arts, and Lane joined WomanKraft in 1975, bringing with her a vision that included theater, dance, music and multimedia art.

Carol Kestler, "WomanKraft at Pima" Workshops and Exhibition, September, 1977

WomanKraft at Pima in September, 1977 was one of WomanKraft's first collaborative shows. The 10-day event at Pima Community College included an art exhibit, a poetry performance by Linn Lane, and a variety of workshops led by WomanKraft artists, including *Presenting Art Photographically* with Carol S. Kestler and N. Skreko Martin (Nancy Martin). Other artists included in the multimedia exhibition were Ann Bannard, Susan Chambers, Eva Cossock, Milky Way, and Ronnye Russell. WomanKraft artists continued to exhibit in a variety of venues, and as they gained visibility they found gallery doors began to inch open to them.

In 1979 the group formed the Community Artists Project (CAP) for the purpose of securing a grant through the federal Comprehensive Employment and Training Act (CETA, 1973-1984), with the CAP operating under the WomanKraft umbrella. Nancy Martin was appointed Project Director and they received funding of up to $90,000 annually until CETA was disbanded in 1984.

The Community Artists Project was Tucson's only CETA-funded visual arts group. Ten artists were initially selected for the program, including Martin, Lane and Gayle Swanbeck, who joined WomanKraft in 1978. They were paid for 20 hours a week for teaching or working on a project,10 hours in the studio, and five hours for meetings, including trainings. During the studio hours the artists had the opportunity to learn about the business end of the artist's lifestyle; preparing portfolios, photodocumenting, creating a resume, and grant writing.

"I learned more about the business of art through WomanKraft than I ever did in college", remarks Swanbeck. An accomplished artist, she also brought her love for teaching into the fold and led classes at various senior and community centers through the CAP. At Tucson House she established the *Young At Art* exhibit showcasing works from senior students, then went on to present the show annually through WomanKraft long after the Community Artists Project had ended.

"Art is therapy," Swanbeck elaborates. "Opening the door to creativity keeps people healthy. For elderly students, art is more than just moving your fingers so the arthritis doesn't bother you. It's a means for keeping busy in an enjoyable way."

"The creative process is for everyone," wrote Linn Lane. "Our intent is to provide a creative experience for people who don't have access to it otherwise."

Gayle Swanbeck and Carol Kestler at Council House, Banner Project.

In 1980 a multimedia group exhibit by the ten artists was installed at the University of Arizona Student Union Gallery. Works by Joy Holdread, Lane, Skreko Martin and Swanbeck were featured among others.

Mural installations were created at the Tucson Association for the Visually Impaired by Gayle Swanbeck and Linn Lane. Other murals were installed at the Pio Decimo Angel Children's Center and through Project Inscape. Mark Lang taught classes on working with clay at the Arizona School for the Deaf and Blind.

"The seeds of WomanKraft's mission and its role as a touchstone were planted during an historic feminist era of creating resources where none had existed before," comments Lavina Tomer, longtime community member. "In the 1970s, Tucson's feminist and lesbian-feminist communities were key in creating shelters, centers, collectives, bookstores, organizations, and university departments."

The Community Artists Project was thriving and the downtown arts district was beginning to flourish as the 1970s, with it's ethic of social progress, rolled over into the '80s, a period that would come to be known as "the decade of greed". Going forward, it would appear WomanKraft never got that memo.

CHAPTER 3

WOMANKRAFT ON CONGRESS STREET, 1981-1991

"Women's Intuition Spring's Initiation Performance"
at Saguaro Monument East, Spring Equinox, March 21, 1981

The Community Artists Project was effective at achieving its goal, getting artists out into the community. Offering instruction in schools and senior centers was one method, and during the summer of 1982 another exciting project took place: the installation of an immense 25'x15 'stoneware tile mural at the Pio Decimo Angel Children Center, 848 South 7th Avenue, Tucson. The project was a collaboration between children attending a summer day camp at the center and artists from WomanKraft.

The installation, dedicated in October 1982, was facilitated by Carol Kestler and N. Skreko Martin. "That was a super project!" Nancy recollects. "The community loved the kid's work on the tiles. We had two bishops at the dedication of the project that was directed by a Pagan and a Jew. It was really interesting that the bishops understood the children's vision-a multireligious perception of a diety in nature."

Joy Holdread, who worked as Skreko Martin's Administrative and Studio Assistant, recollects camping out overnight on-site during the installation. "We'd been working on the tiles all day and they were laid out on the ground," she explained. "There was no way we could just leave them there overnight, so we stayed and kept watch over them. Be sure to mention our brave defense of the tiles," she said, mostly joking.

The mural features the desert sun, A-Mountain and a saguaro. Esther Tang, director of Pio Decimo, conceived of the project as a way to create a lasting monument to the children's contributions. The design was a cooperative conglomeration of their ideas. When Kestler and Skreko Martin asked the students to make sketches that reflected their world, they responded with drawings that included a birthday cake, a thunderstorm and a flower garden. Ceramic masks of the 28 people who helped create the mural, including three community volunteers, four professional artists including Gayle Swanbeck, and 21 children were incorporated. The children were involved in all steps of production, including a visit to Skreko Martin's studio where they were introduced to the processes of glazing and firing. The entire mural was high fired so it would be resistant to rain and sunlight. "It'll last forever," Nancy says.

Funding for the project came from the Tucson/Pima Arts Comission and the Greater Tucson Foundation.

"The Children's Mural" at Pio Decimo Angel Children's Center

During this time Joy Holdread was employed at Project Inscape, the Flowing Wells School District's alternative school for troubled youth. There, in 1983, she facilitated the installation of a 35 square foot stoneware tile mural featuring the faces of 27 students, administrators, faculty members and a board trustee. Making a plaster cast of their face was kind of intense for some; Joy tells about one boy who became claustrophobic, so of course, they removed the plaster pronto. But, after he relaxed and saw how cool the other masks were, he insisted on doing his again. It was a very affirming project for the students.

Photographer Bill Girden documented the installation. Now deceased, Girden photographed many WomanKraft events over the years, and he is missed. Thank you, Bill.

Funding for the project was provided by Abrams Airborne, the Holdread family, and the Fraternal Order of Police.

The Fraternal Order of Police? The way Joy tells it, the artists were holding a meeting in Nancy's dining room one afternoon when the phone rang. Joy answered it and was quiet for a minute, then the table heard her say "Well, actually, I'm thinking you might want to give US some money instead!" She explained about the Project Inscape mural, but no one imagined anything would really come of it. A couple of weeks later, to her surprise, there was a knock on the door and Joy opened it to find an officer with a $500 check in his hand.

Joy Holdread with Students, Project Inscape Mural Installation

By the time the CETA funding ran out the Community Artists Project had identified how strongly Tucson embraced community based art. The women involved were unwilling to let their momentum die off along with the federal monies.

WomanKraft regrouped and began seeking other sources. Nancy Martin served as chief grant writer and, along with Gayle Swanbeck, secured contributions from the Arizona Commission on the Arts, the Grand Foundation, the Chambers family, and the Tucson/Pima Arts Commission (TPAC). Private donations became more vital than ever.

By the early 1980's WomanKraft had developed a reputation for enthusiastically supporting women in the arts, but the organization also had an identity crisis of sorts. Because WomanKraft didn't have a home of its own, people would sometimes assume the exhibitions were presented by whatever building the art was hung in, such as Pima College. Despite this, Martin was still all for showing in alternative spaces, but Lane and Swanbeck were highly motivated for WomanKraft to find its own gallery.

As the Community Artists Project came to a close, interest in video production stepped up. Lane had a cable TV show called *The Woman's Hour* and she collaborated with Phoenix Wheeler and Susie B. on *The Women's Show* on KXCI Community Radio. An on-air reading of her play *The Wiccan Board Meeting* was hosted on the show, as well as other plays, poetry and storytelling events. Linn served as Festival Coordinator for the first Tucson Women's Video Festival in 1984, an event sponsored by the Tucson Women's Cable Consortium which operated under the WomanKraft umbrella.

Third Annual Art Show for Tucson House Art Class, 1984

WomanKraft artists continued reaching out to the community. "In those early years I worked at Keeling Elementary," recalls Debra Jacobson. "I got a grant to have a writer in residence, so I was able to have Linn be there. We had writing workshops and a publishing company. We had these great big magazines. And for every book we published, we made five copies so there would be one for the library, one for the classroom, one to take home, and so on. At the end of the year we had a thing where we traded books. It was great; Linn was a 'real' writer and she was connecting to our students."

Nancy Martin accepted the position of director with the Beth O'Donnell Gallery in 1986 and stepped away from WomanKraft for a few years. After Martin left, Linn Lane assumed the role of WomanKraft Executive Director and the search for a gallery home became top priority. That goal was realized when a lease was secured on a vacant storefront on Congress Street. A tremendous amount of effort was needed to convert the empty space into a gallery, but the artists dove in headlong.

Swanbeck got busy coordinating the thousands of volunteer hours that went into renovations.

Early member Gail Paul recalls building a spiral staircase into the basement with Gayle Swanbeck. The upstairs had the potential to be a airy gallery space with lots of windows and light, but they were lacking a classroom, changing area for performers, and working restrooms on both floors. Additionally, fire codes required two exits from the basement and there was only one.

Conveniently, a round hole was already cut through the main floor so they decided a spiral would be perfect. Using a utility pole, rebar, and some wood they'd found in the basement, Gail and Gayle constructed a beautiful staircase.

There was also the matter of a very heavy, deceased furnace that had to be removed from the basement, and while the women were perfectly willing to tackle most of the jobs the remodel was throwing their way, this one had them stumped. As it happened, their next door neighbor was Johnny Gibson's Gym, and an idea occurred to Linn Lane, who was all of 4'11" and 110 pounds. She went over and asked if there was anyone there who could lift heavy objects?

"She was practically trampled in the doorway," Swanbeck jokes. The bodybuilders made short work of carrying off the old furnace, and kindly checked in often after that to see if they could help with anything else.

Once renovations were complete WomanKraft hit the ground running "We did 10 shows a year in those days," recalls Swanbeck, who was director of exhibits. "A new one every month, except for January and June, when we closed for upkeep. That was a LOT!"

Shortly after the gallery opened, the First Saturday Night Downtown events commenced. WomanKraft held receptions for new exhibits on those evenings, drawing in loads of visitors. Exhibitions during 1986 included the *Women and Girls Primavera Art Exhibit, For Peace Sake, '60's Retrospective, The Elder's Show,* and a *Holiday Bazaar* which would become an ongoing annual event.

Performance arts and concerts quickly took to the stage, as well. Lane was passionate about producing her plays and she plunged into theater presentation, offering her works and original plays by others, as well. "A playwright who has finished writing the play is not finished," she wrote. "The play must be interpreted in readings and/or production."

WomanKraft Developmental Theater formed in 1987 and in '88 presented a series of original and previously unproduced plays and readings by Linn Lane, Madeline Travis, Audrey Ricker, Hannah Blue Heron and others. A variety of events for women were hosted at the gallery, including a series of talks by midwife Maria Cadaxa, a workshop called *Does The Goddess Get P.M.S.?* and a reading of women's erotic short fiction.

Former Arizona State Senator Paula Aboud remembers those performances. "Linn Lane wrote some of the wildest plays," she recalls. "Going to them was great fun! Those were some of the earliest activities of the Tucson women's community, along with the Take Back the Night march and the Pride march. At that time there was no Southern Arizona Aids Foundation (SAAF) and no Wingspan LGBT Center yet. That's my recollection of Linn Lane, she put on these outrageous plays and women just ate them up!"

"It was opportune timing for me that WomanKraft was there when it was," Gail Paul recalls. "I was coming to terms with my own sexuality and artistic abilities. Having like-minded people around that were supportive of women was a powerful experience for me. I felt very lucky to be involved."

Debra Jacobson remembers what it was like working with the charismatic couple of Linn and Gayle in those days. "When they had the gallery on Congress Street, they would have these big fundraising dinners," she recalls. "I was super involved then. Plus, I had a crush on Linn, so that's part of why I was there a lot. Linn was such a wonderful person. She was very powerful in her marvelous, small way. She was so tiny and she had such incredible positive energy. Linn and Gayle's relationship was beautiful. They always had their weekend drive together, and Gayle celebrated their anniversary once a month, every month. They were a lovely couple."

Creative velocity continued to build as WomanKraft entered its second year on Congress Street. One of the highlights of the season was an appearance by multiple Grammy nominee R. Carlos Nakai, the world's premier performer of the Native American flute, who gave his first concert in Tucson at the new gallery.

Other notable events of that year included a psychic fair, concerts featuring Kathleen Williamson, Marty Van der Voort with Andes Chico, and Hannah Blue Heron with Gail Paul; and *The Altar Show*, a one-person exhibit curated by Larry Yáñez. The annual *Young at Art* exhibit initiated by Swanbeck during the Community Artists Project carried on. *People In Cafes*, a portrait drawing workshop, was another of her popular innovations, along with an Art District Tour for children. Linn Lane taught a course on script writing through Pima Community College.

This energetic pace did not falter and the mixed palette of monthly exhibits, original plays, poetry readings, workshops, and concerts carried on into 1988. Lane expanded mixed media productions and established a video library and viewing facility at the Tucson Cable Consortium.

WomanKraft artists installed another ceramic tile mural in 1990, this one at Keeling Elementary School. The work was a collaboration between art teacher Lynn Martinovich and a creative team from WomanKraft. The tile designs were made from pictures drawn by 629 students in the classroom, facilitated by Gayle Swanbeck, who helped the students illustrate their ideas; and from their drawings a tile mural was created for the school. Joy Holdread, along with Landscape Architect Steve Grede, and his partner, Architect Bob Bailey, transferred the images onto clay tiles, then glazed and and fired them. The team installed the mural in a hallway where it still is today.

This project was funded in part by Clarice Margadant, mother of Nan Margadant, president of the board of directors at that time; and by Amphi Schools PTO and Student Council.

Keeling Elementary Mural

Thriving in the Downtown Arts District as the 1980s moved into the '90s, the WomanKraft community was enjoying a high-spirited state of evolution when unexpectedly, disaster struck. Just when it seemed like they'd really hit their stride on Congress Street, an "opportunity" came knocking by way of being forced out by an exorbitant rent increase. Once again, WomanKraft found itself looking for a home. Determined to have their own equity in their own gallery going forward, Lane, Swanbeck and Madeline Travis set out to buy a building.

During six years as the Congress Street cornerstone of the Downtown Tucson Arts District, WomanKraft produced the following: *65 art exhibits, 29 poetry readings, 17 video screenings, 68 musical and 8 dance concerts, 65 workshops, 27 theater productions, 858 art classes, 10 performance art pieces, 15 lectures, and 4 community art projects such as murals. Annual gallery attendance peaked at 65,000 visitors.*

CHAPTER 4

THE LANGUAGE OF ART, GAYLE SPEAKS

Member and Contributing Artist Since 1978

Founder, Director and Instructor of the WomanKraft School of the Arts.

Director of Gallery Exhibits

"Ruins at Hachita" Collage
made of 100% recycled handmade paper

"Landscape West" Collage
made with address labels

Gayle Swanbeck

"I've been thinking about all the things we've done over the years. There have been so many ...

The Tucson arts scene in the 1970s was brutal. There were so many artists and so few places to show. You were relegated to a street fair or some church parking lot; you'd set up at Reid Park and a windstorm would come along and break your art. Rain would come, people wouldn't show up, and every once in a while you'd have a really good show. There are many more places to exhibit now and that's made a big difference.

I joined the Community Artists Project in October 1978. After the grant money ran out we had a core group that was willing to stick it out and we decided we were just going to plow on. We were a volunteer organization; no one was getting any money, but we had committed people at the core and when you have that, you can survive.

Linn and I were willing to 'live without' in order for WomanKraft to survive. It was lucky we saw it the same way. We didn't want children, and we didn't need things; we needed WomanKraft. We needed a place where our art could flourish, and where we could watch other people's art flourish. There's nothing more important than feeling like you're a part of something bigger than yourself. We've had some rough times when we thought we were going to lose everything, but instead we triumphed and grew.

Shortly after CETA funding ended Linn Lane took over the leadership of WomanKraft. No one wanted a repeat of what happened on Congress Street after the ownership of the property passed into the hands of the religious right side of the Carroll family. When they came to look over the building we were having a show about religion and spirituality and it included Wiccan, Jewish, Islamic and Christian art. They were horrified and immediately raised our rent to impossible.

It didn't matter that the gallery had been wildly successful during the six years we'd been there, or that we'd done an extensive remodel of the building (for free). Approximately 700 artists had exhibited at WomanKraft on Congress, but the new owners weren't impressed. When we moved out the space became the Crescent Smoke Shop. After that, Linn's thing was that we needed to buy a building, and there we were, penniless. But Linn said we could do it, and I believed her, and together-with a lot of other people-it happened.

We started offering workshops within six months of relocating to Stone Avenue in '92. I was teaching painting and crafts, and Caroline Latron was doing Reiki massage and French language classes. We officially started calling it the School of the Arts in 1995. Then Linn began publishing the Castle Voice newsletter and we started listing classes, and it just kept growing from there. Now we have a solid core of eight to ten instructors who receive a modest stipend. Occasionally, we're able to offer honorariums for other work as well, but for the most part we're still a volunteer organization.

I think the school will continue on for many years. We always have people who want workshops, and we have teachers. And we'll always have a population of senior students because everyone gets older, and then those people will bring their grandchildren along. When I was younger I used to like instructing older people because it felt like I was surrounding myself with grandparents. Now I'm older and I enjoy mentoring younger people. It's been a nice, full circle.

Our classroom is an intimate art space, and that's what we like about it. We deal mostly with older people, and they've had a lot longer to live with lack of confidence. Many of them don't initially believe in themselves as creative people, but they have a desire. So they can come in and have a one to five ratio with an instructor. It gives them the time they need to get the basis of a craft or an art form. Tuition is free to low income seniors, and supplies are included.

We do trimesters at the School of the Arts, and average 50-60 workshops per session. It's a wide variety. Some of the most popular classes are Ingrid Aspromatis's Wise Women Writing workshop and any of the stained glass mosaic classes.

The ones who come seem to have wonderful times. We've had people who took a workshop and then opened a business, like tile making. The inspirational stories I have are about the moments when people come back to WomanKraft and tell me how it was a significant thing in their life. There's nothing better than that.

The gallery has been a great supporter of community art over the years. Thousands of artists have shown their work at WomanKraft, and about half of the artists at every show are new. Our guidelines for submissions are inclusive; the work needs to fit the theme, and we look at quality. For us, quality has to do with what we see as potential. You can look at a budding artist and know they're going to grow. WomanKraft supports these emerging artists by showing their work.

We've always been successful at reminding people that what we have here is a common language, and that language is art. That's our commonality. You can be different about your identity and the kind of art you make, and still be included here.

We do five exhibits a year now, and two of them are usually new themes. We've been doing the *Drawing Down the Muse* women's show and the *Holiday Bazaar* annually since we were on Congress Street. Other themes vary. The *Black and White and Shades of Gray* show is popular, and it's kind of freeing for artists who work in color to go back to working in black and white. They find it expanding. It makes you look again at space in a way that color doesn't always do.

We've always had huge grassroots support. People who came in for one moment that made the next moments happen. People come and go. They plug in as much as they can, and from the smallest donation of time or money to the largest, these people are what make us go. Even on the rare occasions when we've had people leave under negative circumstances, before things got strange, those people were why WomanKraft survived. They were wonderful until they weren't. You pick up the thread and weave another tapestry.

I hope we can get back to doing events again. I think we can if COVID leaves us alone. The only reason WomanKraft survived during the pandemic was that we already owned the building. We *never* would have been able to come up with a mortgage payment with closed doors for a year and a half! All we had to do was come up with taxes, insurance and utilities. People were very generous to us during COVID, and that has been valuable beyond belief.

I started writing cards and calling people just to check in and see how they were doing, and the result of that human contact was that they donated. We've always been an organization that cared about the people we touched and we keep in contact with them. We've planted trees every year through Tucson Clean and Beautiful to honor docents and financial supporters, about 40 per season. At this point, we've practically planted a forest."

CHAPTER 5

WOMANKRAFT COMES HOME, 1992 -1999

Lydia Phillips fell in love with the Castle on sight. "I was riding the bus to work," she says, "and I saw a for sale sign at the house that is now WomanKraft, and I thought *What a beautiful old house! Somebody needs to make something special out of that.* From what I heard, WomanKraft bought it just two weeks before it was going to be demolished."

Then Madeline Travis, who was on the search committee, spotted it, too. On December 1st, 1992, only 18 days before the building was slated for demolition, WomanKraft put up a $10,000 downpayment donated by Susan Chambers and purchased the 7,840 square foot 1918 Queen Anne Victorian "charmer". Realtor Margaret Koenen volunteered to handle the legal aspects of the purchase.

Located just south of downtown Tucson, the grounds included two freestanding studios, large shade trees and a small parking lot; the enormous yellow house with its eye-catching turret was immediately dubbed "The Castle". The place may have looked quaint from the outside, but inside it was a dilapidated shambles. The rigors of the Congress Street renovation turned out to have been a mere warm-up for what lay ahead on Stone Avenue.

"The original elegance of the property has been diminished by vandalism, transients, and criminal previous attempts at renovations," wrote Linn Lane. "We plan to transform 'The Castle' from a vacant public nuisance into a neighborhood asset."

When they first set foot inside the building it reeked of urine and worse (much worse). Madeline Travis, Caroline Latron and Gayle Swanbeck grabbed shovels and waded in. With two vans and a pickup truck between them, it took 51 trips to the dump before the house was trash-free. Linn Lane and artist Gerrie Young-along with her somewhat dubious teenagers-joined in early on, as well.

"We redid the walls in almost every room," Swanbeck recounts. "We met an older gentleman who was originally from Mexico, and he taught us how to make horse hair plaster. We collected tail clippings, then cut them up and mixed them in. That way the old and new plasters would meld together and hold. The gentleman said 'I've always wanted to find young people who want to learn what I know how to do. I just never thought I'd be teaching it to girls.'"

It appeared their new neighbors approved of their efforts, as well. After Swanbeck had gone to a nearby tile shop to ask if there were any scraps they might part with for an art project, the owner paid a visit and saw the tile mosaic being installed at the front entrance.

"It made me sick they were going to demolish this beautiful old house," he told Gayle. "And look what you girls are doing with it!" The next day a forklift filled with boxes of tiles rumbled up to the Castle.

"We had no idea how we were going to be able to afford to tile the floor," Swanbeck says, "and then, there it was."

She shakes her head over their early naivety. "We thought we would be completely renovated after the first year," she recalls. "It took us two years to even be able open a show!" Since the building had been condemned, everything they did had to be approved by the city, so nothing moved quickly. Boisterous Halloween Haunted Houses filled in for some of the absentee exhibitions during the first two years, and by year three the gallery was open.

Swanbeck didn't waste any time getting classes started, though. She and Latron promptly set up in the freestanding studio in the Castle yard and started teaching. Lydia Phillips was one of their first students.

"To me, it was meant to be," says Phillips. "I was at El Con Mall trying to sign up for a watercolor class and a lady told me that Gayle Swanbeck was an instructor at a location near Grant and Country Club. That's where I met her." To Lydia's delight, the workshops soon moved to Stone Avenue, and she's been taking classes and volunteering ever since.

The history of the house was relayed through word of mouth and by way of Travis's curious daughters, who went downtown to the City Registrar's office and (in a pre-internet world) looked it up on hard copy. They found out that the original owner was a tailor hoping to impress the woman he wanted to marry, but after that it was owned by a series of five single women. Then Dorothy, who'd lived next door since 1920, showed up at a flashlight tour of the Castle and announced they'd all been madams.

According to Dorothy, the house had been an elite brothel until the government started shutting down those sorts of places in the 1940s and '50s. "It's interesting having girls working next door that aren't working girls," she said with a wink.

Gerrie Young adds this bit to Castle history. "It was built by a man hoping to impress a woman, kind of like the Taj Mahal," she jokes. "Then eventually it became a crack house. But because of all that it was ridiculously affordable, and we've worked together to make it what it is now."

By this point WomanKraft's identity had gone through a series of incarnations. First there were the ad hoc installations of the 1970s, then the Community Artists Project of the '80s, followed by the Congress Street Gallery and now, a Castle. Through it all, the intention set by the founding mothers never strayed from its original ethic.

"I think one of the reasons for WomanKraft's longevity is that it has always been community based" says Martin. "Long ago support for the arts came from the Church and the State (monarchy). Then the rich became patrons. Today everyone can be a supporter and a collector. As WomanKraft has become known for supporting emerging artists, it has also become known for affordable art. It responds to its community. Also, you need to get collectors addicted at an early age, and affordability is one way of doing that.

"WomanKraft was founded so that women would have a place to show their work, and the association of the gallery with the School of the Arts is symbiotic," Martin points out. "Some people who view art are interested in the process, and some artists are interested in supplementing their incomes by demonstrating and teaching."

"And when you buy art from WomanKraft," Swanbeck adds pragmatically, "your money goes back into your community."

WomanKraft artists being taped for a program about Downtown Arts District projects, to be aired by the Tucson Community Cable Corporation. Linn Lane is explaining the WomanKraft mural installation in Arizona Alley on the wall of Cafe Magritte. Fun fact: two of the tiles were created by Senator John McCain and Congressman Jim Kolbe, who were Downtown Arts District tourists on the day the tiles were made. Clockwise around the table from the back: Linn Lane, Gayle Swanbeck, Joanne Pritzen, Caroline Latron, Nicole Young, Gerrie Young, Madeleine Travis.

While WomanKraft may have stayed true to the original vision of the founders, the landscape shifted pretty dramatically for the art center in other ways after the move from Congress Street. Obviously, an enormous Victorian-era house in need of extensive remodeling was going to cost a lot more than the modest gallery space they'd leased downtown, and by the mid-1990s only about 14% of operating costs were still being covered by city and federal grant monies. Private and corporate donations became more important than ever; Susan Chambers and her mother Freda Macadam Chambers were strong advocates of community based art and loyal supporters of WomanKraft throughout their lives. Susan's brother Wid, an artist himself, has funded this history. Freda Chambers sponsored the addition of the handicapped access ramp into the building in 1994.

Corporate sponsors included the Grand Foundation, IBM, Cafe Magritte, Cocos, Huntington Trading Company, Berta Wright Gallery, and Sasabe Tile Company. Public funding for the years 1994-1995 was also given by the Community Development Block Grant administered through the City of Tucson, which donated $20,000 for building repairs.

'Roses', Mixed Media Drawing   *Floral Bouquet', Mixed Media Drawing*

Susan Chambers

Another difference in the new location was that they were no longer on the beaten path of the Downtown Arts District, so they weren't getting the hefty number of visitors from foot traffic they'd enjoyed on Congress Street. On the other hand, the space was ideal for classes and the School of the Arts prospered in its new home. Receptions, exhibitions and special events drew people in. Slowly but surely, the building was being restored to the magnificence of earlier days; and so it was that the WomanKraft Castle grew into a landmark and a destination.

One particularly memorable event of 1995 was the mother/daughter exhibition *Figures and Fabrics* by Freda Macadam Chambers and Susan Chambers. "Susan's mother was a blue-chip painter," says Nancy Martin. "She showed at Covington Gallery and she had a one-person show at the Tucson Museum of Art." In her autobiography *Freda*, Macadam Chambers mentions that as a young woman, she was the first female artist invited to enter a painting in a World's Fair. She displayed in the 1939 American Art exhibit in New York City.

A prodigious talent in her own right, Susan's media was fabric dying and embellishment, which she learned while studying in Japan with the National Living Treasure, Serizawa. Susan and her husband, photographer Art McGregor, had a combined exhibition in 1999. Tragically, Susan passed away earlier that year due to surgical complications following a prolonged illness, and that became a memorial show. Susan was a great champion of the arts in Tucson and is sorely missed to this day.

Nancy Martin was able to increase her involvement with WomanKraft when her position as director of another gallery ended in

1996, and she returned as an organizer of the *Drawing Down the Muse* conferences. She took on the roles of chief grant writer and secretary for the board of directors, where she has remained working quietly behind the scenes ever since.

Photo by Barbara Cooper

The first *Drawing Down the Muse, An International Conference for Women* in 1996 defined the event as annual, and it was presented through 2008. The theme was *The creative process and nurturing your life as a woman and artist*. Nancy Martin led the workshop *Marketing Your Art* and Gerrie Young facilitated a session called *Environmental Symbol Searching For*

Spiritual Sacredness. There were workshops about dreams, visual expression, the creative process and more.

An exhibition celebrating *Women Artists Return From the Darkness* was held in conjunction with the conference. Exhibiting artists included:

Susan Chambers, Silkscreening

Judy Chicago, Mixed Media Print

To-Ree-Nee Keiser, Painter/ Mixed Media

Linn Lane, Collaborative Mixed Media

Caroline Latron, Stained Glass Mosaics

N. Skreko Martin, Sculpture

Giga Soto, Drawing

Gayle Swanbeck, Drawing/Handmade Paper Collage

Gerrie Young, Sculpture, Pastel Drawing

For the second year of the conference in 1997, Gerrie Young led the workshop *Intercultural Arts.* "Often we are able to overcome difficulty in dealing with people in other ethnic groups by learning something about the art, life-styles and spiritual influences in their lives," she wrote. Participants were able to use materials such as inks and block cuts that are unique and used in only a few cultures.

Getting in Synchronicity with Our Creative Animals by Cat Spencer, *Getting Writing Published* with Lusia Slomkowska and *Finding Meaning in Life's Transitions* by Susannah Fiering were some of the other workshops offered that year.

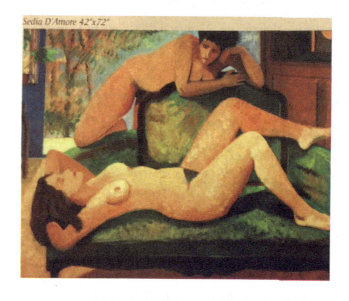

Sedia D'Amore 42"x72"

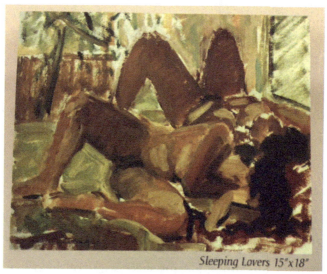

Sleeping Lovers 15"x18"

Paintings by Lorraine Inzalaco

The groundbreaking one-woman exhibition *Visible for a Change* by outspoken lesbian artist Lorraine Inzalaco came to the gallery in 1999. "In order for values and creativity to flourish, we must have our Lesbian art," Inzalaco wrote. "Although there have been many Lesbian artists through history, most of them were erased by homophobic and misogynistic art librarians. We must have the right to decide for ourselves what our public images are to be."

The lesbian images painted by Inzalaco exude sensuality and a gentle eroticism; her women lie in bed together satisfied, or in one case, alone reclining on a bench next to a dildo. "I believe it is essential for everyone, not just Lesbians, to see beautiful images of women loving each other through a Lesbian's eyes. It is only through this conversation that we start to see ourselves as members of the world beyond or own enclaves," Inzalaco concluded.

After a few years in the Castle, Linn Lane's considerable imagination saw yet another possibility for the space besides gallery, theater, art school, concert hall, conference center, haunted house, karaoke den, art studios, and bed and breakfast: She wanted retail!

Anubis's Hideaway was a little shop tucked into a room at the back of the Castle where Linn did Tarot and other spiritual readings. The shop carried cards, candles, oils, incense and wall hangings. At an open house in July, 1998, some of the presentations offered were astrology, practical magic, wand making, ritual creation, and a talk by an ordained pagan minister who counseled alien abductees.

Lydia Phillips remembers meeting Terri McGuire at those early painting classes with Gayle. "People come and go," she says, "but sometimes you see a loyalty to WomanKraft. Sometimes people get on board, and stay on board." The two of them certainly did. Phillips went on to become president of the board of directors, a key volunteer with the annual rummage sale and other projects, and a perpetual student of the arts.

WomanKraft School of the Arts Workshop: 'Once Junk' workshop and recycled paper making
Gayle Swanbeck, instructor

Terri McGuire credits the arts group for helping her to discover not only her artistic talent but a much improved self-image. She recalls finally gathering her courage to bring a piece in for an exhibit. "For the first time, I felt like I was doing what I was supposed to be doing," she says. "I felt like I came home when I got involved with WomanKraft. The Castle is alive, it's made up of all of us."

CHAPTER 6

SACRED DOLLS, GERRIE SPEAKS

Gerrie Young, Member and Contributing Artist Since 1993

Instructor, School of the Arts

'Gardener Cat' Raku-fired ceramic plaque 7" X 10", Gerrie Young

"I've been involved with WomanKraft for 30 years. We had been in the Air Force all through my husband's career, and Arizona is one place that people spoke badly of, but I've always had a good time here. When my husband retired here, it was like, What am I going to do with these teenage kids? What am I going to do with myself, I don't know anybody. I thought this far west was way beyond where we wanted to be, but we're going to make the best of it, and we're going to find things to do.

I saw Gayle's picture in the Tucson Weekly and she was asking for volunteers. I said that's a good place to start, why don't we see what this is, and how we can help? So one of the first things I did was take my kids downtown, because I wanted to find somewhere to show my work. I make ceramic sculpture and I also make intaglio prints.

I wasn't thinking about that when I went to WomanKraft, though; I was just thinking it was a place for artists to go and help out. If I could show somebody my work, that was fine, and if not; well, that was fine, too. But, I would be in a group of people that understood what I was into. Then Gayle invited me to show my work at WomanKraft, and that's how I got started.

When my kids saw the house they thought *My mom's absolutely crazy. But she's gonna take us there anyway.* Everything there was something good for them to learn: fixing a wall, putting down tiles, sweeping the floor, building a house. That's how it turned into 30 years, because there was always something for me to help with and I liked that. And I needed sisters, because I have five sisters and they all live in Philadelphia.

Creative Weekend
Left to right: Lois Stewart, Gayle Swanbeck, Quynn Elizabeth, Linn Lane.
Gerrie Young is in foreground wearing gold headband.

The *Drawing Down the Muse* Conference in 1996 was one of the things that made me think WomanKraft was the best place for me to be, and a place for women from all different walks of life to come together. We had to get out of our own medium and join into other areas of art. I went to a group where we divided up into dancing, writing, poetry, and painting, and you could join in on any of those. The people that came really appreciated trying different things.

Another time, after we'd gotten the house fixed up enough to actually be able to have something there, we had a Halloween Haunted House night where Linn Lane was doing seances and Tarot readings. The whole place was a maze, and the beauty shop was a graveyard. It was hilarious! And we had poetry readings upstairs. That's how it is at WomanKraft; something really special happens, and then you keep hanging in there, waiting for something else great to come along and take place.

I also liked the theater. Linn and Gayle put on several performances, and so did Dan and Paul with Speak the Speech Theater. Linn was actually pretty ill at the time. But the presentations turned out very well, so it was nice being there. Since Linn passed away we haven't been doing much as far as the performance arts.

Linn was a force to deal with, let me tell you! I remember she had her little shop, Anubis's Hideaway, and I'm a shopper so it was fun to go in there. We were friends; I miss her a lot. She had a different point of view and she was quite a writer. She was on TV a lot promoting WomanKraft, and she did ads and interviews on the radio. Linn was great.

I've been involved with most of the exhibitions in one way or another, either with a submission or helping to hang the show. WomanKraft caters to everybody; we never turn down a person that wants to have a try at making art and exhibiting. There are a lot of high end art places where you have to be very polished to get in. WomanKraft gives people an opportunity to just try it and see if art is a good fit for them.

I'm also an instructor with the WomanKraft School of the Arts. I have a Sacred Dolls class and a watercolor class. Sacred Dolls is a community class where people come together and talk about what sacredness is to them. What is really special to you? How do you make something that shows the sacred power these objects have? We do affirmations about making art, and understanding that you can make art with anything. Then you make this sculptural doll to show that. It's about empowering people to move forward and choose things that are going to remind them of how special they are.

We were very happy to be back after the pandemic. There was a good turnout at the first exhibit, and people were very careful, everybody had masks on. Then we had this other night where people that knew each other from a long time ago came and had tea and crumpets. They came back to WomanKraft to meet up again after COVID. It was nice!

I think WomanKraft's greatest accomplishment is bringing people together that probably otherwise would never get together. It gathers all this community and says 'You're welcome to come in and look around'."

CHAPTER 7

AN ARTIST AND A GODDESS, TERRI SPEAKS

Terri McGuire,
Member and Contributing Artist Since 1993.
Instructor, School of the Arts and
Former Co-Director of Exhibits.
Former President, Board of Directors.s

African Oasis Sunrise

"I got involved with WomanKraft in the mid '90s when I signed up for an oil painting class. I walked into the main building, which we call the Castle, and I felt like the house embraced me. It was a sad time in my life. I was going through a lot of personal stuff, and it became a haven for me. I could go there and interact with people I had never encountered before, and they didn't care who I was or where I came from; they just accepted me and said 'Hey, let's talk about art'.

When I started going to WomanKraft life was really chaotic for me. My marriage was in bad shape; my job wasn't going well; my son was really little. Everyone was so accepting of who I was, and who I didn't even know I was. I was whoever everybody else thought I should be.

I got here and we were doing oil painting, and Gayle said to me, 'You know Terri, you're really an artist.'

I said. 'Oh no, I'm not!' I come from a family of artists, and I've never felt like I measured up to the rest of them. Then I saw a project Gayle had recently finished: a group of statuettes of Venus of Willendorf, a fertility goddess, and I realized I was built just like her! My body was unacceptable to every significant male person in my life, especially my husband, and I looked at those and thought Wow, people worshipped her? Then I researched her and I couldn't believe it.

We had a show coming up and I decided to make a piece for it. It was a Dia de los Muertos theme. It sold before the show even opened! Again, Gayle said 'Terri, you're an artist!' The longer I was there, the more I learned about different points of view and started finding out who I was. I learned to accept and love myself. Today I can tell you that I am an artist AND I am a Goddess!

I've been a WomanKraft student, a live model, and a docent for the gallery. I was president of the board of directors for a while. Now I'm co-coordinator of exhibits with Gayle, and I'm training to take over running the gallery, but I still have a fulltime job. I retire in five years.

Something I've discovered that's a challenge for me is that when deciding what to accept for exhibits, I have to set my personal judgment aside. Just because I may not particularly care for a piece doesn't necessarily mean it's not good for the show. I have to look at the artwork in a different way, and that's exciting for me.

Gayle was the Director of Exhibits and the Director of the School of the Arts, and after Linn died she took on the entire mantle, except Nancy Martin does the grant writing. I'm learning how to do Gayle's job (but not the grant writing). It can't just be one person who bears the brunt of everything. It's always worked better when there were two people in charge.

WomanKraft has been in Tucson for 50 years and in the Castle for 30 years, and we fill a vital niche in Tucson. We've helped hundreds, if not thousands, of artists get started. I like to think it's because we're so accepting of people. We try to support folks in finding their strong areas and developing those.

This is truly where my heart is. I feel like I'm doing exactly what I'm supposed to be doing. WomanKraft is very down to earth and very eclectic. These folks are real."

CHAPTER 8

A CREATIVE SURGE, 2000-2009

Arts of all sorts decked the halls of the Castle as the 1990s swiveled into a new millennium. Developmental Theater, Storytelling Brigade, poetry readings, gallery exhibits, receptions, live music, Tarot readings and more were happening on South Stone Avenue.

The looming "Y2K" had a lot of people concerned that their computer software would crash when the clock struck the year 2000, but at WomanKraft, where operations had stayed intentionally low tech, nobody gave that a second thought.

The gallery kicked off spring 2000 with *The Altar Show, An Exhibit of Altar and Shrine Installations*. The May reception included a Ceremony for the Earth, led by Zelima Xochiquetzal, Nicaraguan Curandera (healer). Gayle Swanbeck recalls a 3' long wing feather from an Andes Mountain Condor she used to bless the room, along with white sage and tobacco.

Much beloved WomanKraft artist Ana Yañez led the workshop *Paper Flowers* in 2001, demonstrating the traditional Mexican craft of making crepe paper and tissue flowers. Ana found her way to WomanKraft through a Downtown Art Walk in the mid-1990s, where Linn Lane pointed her in the direction of the studio out back where Gayle's painting class had just let out.

Ana told Gayle she loved art and making things and so, of course, she was invited to join the class. "It quickly became clear she was very talented," Swanbeck recalls. "When I first started working with her I noticed some of her techniques were better than mine, methods she'd learned as a girl growing up in Mexico. So I turned some of my workshops over to her."

Yañez has been an inspiration to other artists because of the way she came to embrace art later in life. She was a woman who'd moved to a strange country for her husband, then found herself divorced with small children to raise. She taught herself English, found a job and made it work. It wasn't until she was in her 60s that she was able to grow the seed of art she'd been harboring all those years. She'd been creating folkloric pieces that she sometimes sold in craft fairs at St. Margaret's church, but when Ana connected with WomanKraft, her talent shifted from a hobby to a way of life.

She has continued to submit art for shows and teach workshops for many years. In a holiday card she sent to the board of directors when she was 91 years old and no longer able to continue coming in person, Ana wrote "Without WomanKraft I never would have been where I am today, with my art and my peace of mind."

One standout exhibit for the ages, as far as Nancy Martin is concerned, was *Glob-all: Young Polish Women Photograph Their World*, curated by 32 year-old Polish Photographer Katarzyna Majak in 2002. Martin and Majak met by chance at a photography workshop at the Atlantic Center for the Arts in Florida, where they saw a poster requesting proposals for exchanges between artists from the United States and Eastern Europe.

It took two years and funding from a variety of sources to make it happen, but when it finally did, the exhibit featured Majak's work and that of three other Polish photographers. Their photographs are taken through the eyes of the first generation to grow up under democracy rather than communism, making this a unique type of exhibit. Martin was interested to learn that the young artist thought women enjoyed more equality under communism than when the Polish Catholic Church came back in force and began urging women to marry, stay home and have babies.

Desert Leaf magazine quotes Majak as saying that it's photography's "omnipresence, its power, its magic" that has held her attention. "There is always something new to discover and the best pictures are usually taken when you forget the rules," she remarked.

Music filled the halls in those years, as well. Singer-Songwriter Lilla Luoma rocked the little Castle stage with Dave Porter on bass and Andes Chico on drums in March, 2005. The playbill for the show described Luoma's music as "a unique blend of folk, rock, country and blues, interlaced with a sense of ancient and modern cultural mystery." Luoma also provided musical scores for Lane's plays *Guru Genoa* and *Waters Edge*.

Sadly, Luoma passed away from cancer several years later. She is deeply missed.

One of the most exciting productions of the decade was Linn Lane's play "Water's Edge" when it was mounted at the Procenium Theater at Pima College in 2007. This was a major accomplishment for Lane, as it was for Director Swanbeck and the actors.

"To finally put on one of her productions with all of the bells and whistles that a real theater can give you; lighting, special effects, seating ... wow," says Swanbeck. "We saw her play the way it was meant to be seen, on a big stage. It was a fantastic experience, and really wonderful for Linn."

Lane was a prolific playwright and she also made full production videos that were aired on Channel 9, PBS and community access cable TV. WomanKraft put on a multitude of plays, not just Linn's but other peoples' as well, giving many people their first opportunities. According to Swanbeck, they produced 16 of Lane's plays over the years.

The school was expanding and the gallery enjoying a creative surge as the first decade of the 21st century made its way into the next. Social climate seemed to be edging towards the more equitable: the United States elected its first Black president, Barack Obama, that year and Iceland elected Johanna Siguroadottir, its first female and openly lesbian prime minister.

On South Stone Avenue, WomanKraft continued to do what it had always done as 2010 rolled in, pushing the boundaries of the conventional through art.

CHAPTER 9

LINN LANE'S AUTOBIOGRAPHY

Written by Linn Lane, 1999

Linn Lane, Member 1976-2012

WomanKraft Executive Director 1986-2012

Deceased 2012

Poet, Playwright, Administrative Director of WomanKraft, a Multi-media Arts Center. Also video writer, director and editor.

I was born in the natural sign of writers, Gemini, in the Colorado village of Bayfield. I grew up there and in a couple of other Colorado and New Mexico small towns.

I learned to read and write before I went to school and this plus my mothers bedtime stories made my life bearable. I discovered Susan B. Anthony at 9 and got my first feminist awakening. I read all the books in the library. My father, who hadn't finished 8th grade was in awe of my mother's college degree but he did not appreciate the connection between my literacy and my imagination. Where I lived creativity was not considered a virtue.

Trees, rivers, and animals were my best friends. I developed a great capacity for isolation.

College was escape. I worked all the time but finally ended up with a Psychology degree. Later I got other papers in media and administration.

The feminist movement of the 70s and the emerging Woman-identified poets catalyzed me into reading the poetry I'd always hidden. This happened in 1974 in Tucson, Arizona. Around then I became friendly with a group of women visual artists who were in the process of forming a nonprofit corporation to claim and validate women artists called WomanKraft. At this time women in all the arts were almost guaranteed to not be included in important expositions.

I wanted to be part of WomanKraft but I was a writer/performer not a visual artist. My process was to write poems, mini dramas, and other narratives and then create voices, visual effects, and confrontations to connect with an audience. These methods became known generally as "Performance Art". I didn't have a name for it.

In 1976 I was in the middle of a big performance featuring 15 women at a National Organization of Women conference when the microphones went dead. I was astonished to learn that the president of N.O.W., who had invited me, had decided to shut off the power because an older lady had complained about the language used in the piece. I was devastated. My friends at WomanKraft wrote a letter to N.O.W. explaining why freedom of expression is important for the Women's Movement too. They also let me join WomanKraft and changed the philosophy to include all types of artists. I will always be grateful.

Playwriting was a natural progression of my attempts to make my work more visual and kinetic. At this time, 1996, I have written seven full length and several shorter plays. I have produced all but the latest.

In 1979 WomanKraft got a Comprehensive Education and Training Grant to employ artists. I was one of the ten selected and became the multi-media consultant for the group. An innovation of the plan was that we could learn whatever we thought we needed most to know and the grant paid for the training involved. I began learning video.

Programs I've made include two full-length features from my play scripts, two documentaries, and some interviews with women artists. My current project is an experimental piece using poetry.

In 1985 I became the director of WomanKraft and was instrumental in getting our organization's first truly public space, a victory of women's cultural visibility. Before this time we had operated out of what we called alternative spaces. This meant that while we didn't have regular rent payments to make, our events were often perceived as being those of the organization whose space we were using. The space we leased was in the downtown, an area inhabited mostly by drunks, and required total renovation. The rent was reasonable. We made the building beautiful, useable, and created a friendly risk-taking environment. We were early pioneers in creating what is now called Tucson's Arts District. One year we saw 65,000 visitors.

At the end of the next year, 1992, our lease was not renewed at our affordable rate. The new owners of the building didn't like feminists. Also, the area was commercially developed now, thanks to us and others like us and so the owners could get more rent than what we paid.

What happened next is magic. There has always been magic in my life. WomanKraft members met and affirmed that we intended to continue a public venue, in the Arts district and that furthermore that this space would be WomanKraft owned not rented and would in every way be better.

On December 1,1992, I signed the papers to buy our current home for the arts, "The WomanKraft Castle," a huge, Queen Anne Victorian that provides us with adequate gallery, studio, and educational space. It has wonderful grounds with huge trees, six kinds of lizards, 12 kinds of butterflies, humming birds. It is the kind of place one dreams of returning to. When we obtained it a lot of people called it more of a nightmare than a dream. It had been abandoned for several years, the back yard was a trash heap, the inside smelled terrible and was also full of garbage. Nothing worked and previous renovations were criminal. The city was threatening to demolish the building as a health hazard. People said we were crazy to go where professionals feared to tread.

We did and are still doing the renovations ourselves. Now people say how lucky we are to have such a great building. They just don't understand how a group of such poor women artists came to own a Castle.

CHAPTER 10

WISE WOMEN WRITING, INGRID SPEAKS

Ingrid Aspromatis, Member Since 2008

Instructor, School of the Arts

Gallery Docent

"I found WomanKraft by happenstance in 2008. I was at a restaurant across the street and we noticed there was something going on; it turned out there was a reception that evening. We walked over to check it out and I immediately fell in love with the concept and with the lovely people there. Thats how it started. Happenstance or fate, who knows?

The first time I met Linn Lane she walked up to me with open arms. We totally clicked. She was like a piece of *light*. I never heard any negative criticism from her; she would look at something and there was always a solution. If she could help someone, she would. Linn was a truly idealistic person who lived it; she walked her talk. She was a bubble of energy; some people just have extra, you know? And they know how to spread that to others and uplift them. She was like a fairy sprite, I always looked for her wings. She was this tiny, big force, the mouse that roared.

I can't believe she's been gone for so many years. She passed in 2012 and now there's only few of us left that actually knew her. It was a big blow to lose her and there was a lot of sorrow. It was hard to see her health deteriorate, but she was positive to the end.

I loved the way Gayle and Linn worked in tandem. They had skills in different areas and they complimented each other. I have to tell you, Gayle is incredible. I wish I had some of her brain cells; I think she has extra. She is amazing in her abilities, in her strength and devotion. She's high functioning and smart, and she knows how to organize. You can see WomanKraft is like her child. She's still the big force, lubricating the wheels and keeping it going.

I've been facilitating the Wise Women Writing workshop since 2008 and we meet once a month. It has appeal on a lot of different levels; there's a real intimacy in sharing writing. I'm happy facilitating my workshop because I know it's helped people and changed lives. Many women have told me it's been very therapeutic to write like that and share it in a safe place.

Bernabe Garcia, Yaqui Elder, teaching gourd rattles for WomanKraft School of the Arts.

And the School of the Arts! All these wonderful, diverse classes that we offer at such a reasonable price; people flip out over that. There are mosaics classes, a drumming workshop, painting with oil sticks … Jordana, who has the salon, teaches the techniques of how to do a pedicure. The classes are constantly changing. A $20 workshop for two hours, that's fabulous, right? Over the years, many women have been inspired to create art and then go on to exhibit. They weren't artists when they first came to WomanKraft, but they learned skills and, with encouragement, started creating art. Isn't that lovely? There's a personal touch at WomanKraft you don't find everywhere.

I've been a gallery docent for the past five years. My husband James Aspromatis volunteers, too; he hangs pictures for the shows. It's enjoyable for both of us because we get to do that together. It's a great feeling to be of service and to promote WomanKraft and help keep it going. A lot of us are aging out, though. I'm 74. My health is pretty good, so I'm going to stay active as long as I can. I believe in WomanKraft; it's unique in all of Tucson.

I think the key to WomanKraft's longevity is that it provides not only opportunity, but also a sense of community. It brings like-minded people together that have a certain altruism and who want to support this mission. We provide space for artists that would not have another venue readily available. I love that I can go to the Castle and be around people of consciousness. WomanKraft gives the opportunity for exposure to other artists, and you have the chance to socialize with progressive thinkers who believe in things like science and women's rights. It makes a difference. WomanKraft is such a treasure, and I'm happy to be a part of keeping it alive. I think it attracts special people, and what's not to like about art?"

Ingrid Aspromatis (back row, far right) leads the popular "Wise Women Writing" workshop.

CHAPTER 11

A BEAUTIFUL, AMORPHOUS CREATURE, ZOE SPEAKS

Zoe Rhyne, Member and Contributing Artist 2010-2021

Co-director of Exhibits 2017-2019

Director of Exhibits 2019-2021

Josh Smith and Zoe Rhyne
Photo Credit Ellen Parrish

"My sister Grace and I had decided we were going to try to do the artist thing. We were very young; she was 17 and I was almost 19. We'd made a bunch of crafts and art and were selling at a Second Saturday Downtown. We only sold one thing, but we had six people say to us,

'Have you tried WomanKraft? Your stuff would be perfect there.' The next day we scheduled an appointment with Gayle and she accepted us into the *Holiday Bazaar*. We joined in November 2010 and dove in headfirst from that point on.

We were doing mostly mixed media and had a lot of shadow box kinds of things. We were just making stuff to make stuff; we were deep into the crafting phase of our journey. The art we're doing now is pretty much the same, only more refined. That was an advantage I got from WomanKraft, I got to explore so many different mediums. I was able to discover what I liked best and what liked me the best.

That's the thing about art, sometimes you wish you could do a realistic watercolor portrait, but you just can't. It's easier not to get discouraged when you have options because you can try it a different way.

When we first started Gracie and I became docents for the gallery and in exchange for that we got to rent Studio #102 at a reduced rate. It was very interesting, because having a space dedicated to making art makes a difference; it's not like you're making a big mess on your kitchen table and then you have to clean it up every day before you cook dinner.

Studio #102
Photo by Barbara Cooper

WomanKraft made art into more of a reality for us. We were babies shooting in the dark, so it was interesting to be confronted with the idea you could be an artist and that's what you were. It wasn't, 'Oh, I work at this job and I also make art.' It was, 'This is what I do.' There was never any false hope it was going to be easy. It wasn't, 'You'll be an artist and then you'll be selling $1000 paintings in no time.' It was, 'You'll be an artist, but you're going to have to be scrappy.'

We learned that you have to advertise your skills in multiple ways and you have to figure out what you can do with them. I made more money teaching art than I ever did selling art. Sharing art with people in that way was very special. I enjoyed teaching, and I took that bull by the horns pretty hard.

If you could make a piece of art and had the supplies for it, you could teach a class at the School of the Arts. It was fun to be able to teach a variety of things. For instance, if somebody donated a pile of vases that looked the same, what workshop could we do with those? Mixed media art can be any combination of painting and collage and assemblage. 'Media' in art is anything: watercolor, photography, poetry. It's a big word.

Gayle taught me how to do stained glass and that was just like, 'Oh man, this is it!' We did stained glass mosaics, which was much simpler than stained glass with leading and soldering. You still learned to cut and shape glass, and to think about negative space in a different way, and the way that colors can be used to make something. My favorite part was seeing how everybody started with the same instruction and supplies and then made something so different. It's a peek into the human psyche that's fascinating, and it's fun to feed off of each other's creativity.

The School of the Arts offers scholarships to low income people over 50, so it's specifically geared towards adults. Many people have never given themselves the opportunity to do art, because it's such a frivolous thing in our society's view. To see someone make something that came out the way they wanted it to, and have them be satisfied with it, was awesome.

When you're told it's something that doesn't matter and why are you wasting your time, art seems so frivolous. But when you are told it does matter, and someone recognizes that you have been so vulnerable as to put yourself on the wall and say 'Judge me!', that's an extraordinary thing. Helping people realize they, too, can do art is beautiful.

I think making art accessible to everyone, whether it's creating it or buying it, is the goal our society should have overall. WomanKraft embodies that ideal perfectly. Everybody speaks art.

Josh Smith, my partner, was there the whole time, too. He became an active artist, and he stayed busy putting the Castle back together. He repaired pretty much every single room and repainted the entire outside of the building. Josh did any and all maintenance; he built the stage and made the gorgeous winged fence in the front. I don't think there's one room that doesn't have Josh in it. The priorities were set by Gayle, and he did them. Josh almost single-handedly brought that old girl back to life.

WomanKraft gave Josh a chance to explore a creativity that, as a boy growing up in Marana, was not necessarily encouraged. He's always been an incredibly capable welder and when we went to WomanKraft he got to explore the art side, as well.

Left to right: Jaynie Anguliano, Grace Rhyne, Samantha Transue, Tadeo Valdez-Celaya Of Esperanza Dance Project.

When we first joined Linn was still with us. Grace is very detail oriented; her label maker has a label on it that says "label maker", so she and Linn bonded over that. Linn was teaching her about being an executive director and I was being mentored by Gayle with the School of the Arts and the gallery in mind. I apprenticed for two and a half years before I received the full title. Before I started apprenticing, I helped hang the shows, so I was there as a witness when Gayle was doing it. It was great to learn from doing instead of just reading a book.

Once I became director of exhibits one of the best things was choosing the themes for the shows. Every artist would interpret it differently, and it was cool to see what everybody would bring. You had to have something broad enough you could get a wide array of artists, but specific enough you could tell there was a theme to the show. I liked listening to peoples' explanations of how their work fit.

You have to be careful with things like abstract art though, because not every piece actually has to be about the relationship you had with your mother. But you do have to be feeling something, even if that feeling is *I thought these two colors went together really well*. At least you're putting thought into it.

We knew Linn for far too little of a time. We were only involved with WomanKraft for about six months before she passed. We went into it fast because there was a big power vacuum. (Power isn't quite the right word.) We needed to fill a lot of roles very quickly, and Grace and I were willing to help in any way we could. Nancy and Gayle were eager to find another generation they could teach things to. We learned how to do everything: taxes, grant writing, hanging shows, organizing fundraisers. We learned there were a lot of things to be done and a lot of opportunity to do them.

Grace was with us for almost seven years, then she left to pursue a college degree and other interests. She was doing a lot with Saffos Dance Theater, and she was also in the Esperanza Dance Project. She had filled a huge administrative role and a lot of that fell back on the shoulders of those of us who were still there. That was hard.

Gayle Swanbeck is a force, a gale force, right!? She was a wonderful mentor, a very good teacher, and is an incredibly talented artist. She has always maintained her commitment to WomanKraft, which is beyond reproach.

I will say also, Nancy Martin is a secret pillar for WomanKraft that most people don't even know is holding it up. She is our last involved founding mother, and she's a *badass*. I wanna BE Nancy when I grow up; she's amazing! She is an incredible artist who recognized what WomanKraft had to offer to the community, and she really embraced that. Nancy taught me everything I know about grant writing. She's still there, despite everything, no matter what.

I think the key to WomanKraft's longevity is that the founding mothers were amazing in their forethought when they incorporated in the 70s. It was built on the foundation of art for everyone by a bunch of women who were sick of being told there was no space for them, so they made their own space. When they wrote the bylaws they were so open about it they didn't choke WomanKraft into doing only one thing.

WomanKraft is a beautiful, amorphous creature that can be and is many things for many people. The building itself isn't narrowed down into being only an art gallery, or only a dance performance space.

The organization has survived tumultuous, unthinkable times, and going forward WomanKraft can change into whatever it needs to be. There's infrastructure there already to continue for a long time. The infrastructure is a big deal, because building an audience is difficult and building a name for yourself, almost impossible. The fact it's been in the same place for so long means people know where it is and they're familiar with it. That makes a big difference.

I would say WomanKraft's greatest accomplishment is giving a voice to women and other under represented people and letting them know that art matters. Our society does a huge disservice thinking the only values that are important are math and science and being a doctor. Not that those are not important, but art is the way our souls communicate."

Winged Gate by Josh Smith

CHAPTER 12

A STEADY HEARTBEAT, 2010-2019

Despite its state of persistent optimism, WomanKraft had seen its share of tragedy along the way, and another one struck in 2012. After an eight year struggle with Chron's disease, we lost Linn Lane. She left behind scores of loved ones and admirers who still can't quite imagine the world on its proper axis without her, as well as volumes of her works. The WomanKraft community was devastated, as was the Tucson arts community. Linn is greatly missed.

The Castle is her beautiful legacy. Since no one has reported any mysterious floating lights or art moving around randomly, she doesn't seem to be haunting the place. Still, there's a feeling of her in the halls and on the stage, and I can tell you this: Linn Lane has been looking over my shoulder the entire time I've been writing this book about her beloved WomanKraft. Every once in a while she finds a word I've lost and brings it back to me.

Everyone grieved for Linn in her own way. Ultimately, the greatest way to honor her was to keep WomanKraft alive and growing, and so the shows went on.

The nonprofit Speak the Speech Theater was incorporated in 2014 by Dan Reichel and Paul Brunnel with the purpose of inspiring "the willingness to generate dialogues concerning class, justice, and the courage to explore our own humanity." The company produced *True West* by Sam Shepard, and other plays. Reichel had also acted a major role in Lane's play *Water's Edge* in 2007. Speak the Speech Theater operated out of the WomanKraft Castle for five years.

By this point the gallery had a steady heartbeat of four annual exhibitions, two rummage fairs, and the *Holiday Bazaar*. The same stability was true of the School of the Arts and its 50-class trimesters. Swanbeck and Martin were becoming increasingly interested in training their replacements. Grace Rhyne assumed the role of executive director in 2014, and Zoe Rhyne began training with Gayle on gallery operations. Josh continued painting, polishing and constructing improvements to the Castle.

There was a lot of good energy about, and the Castle was hopping in 2014 with activities like Karaoke, pumpkin carvings, art raffles and a variety show. Studio rentals were made available, and the web site was upgraded. Work began on increasing social media presence.

It was reported at the board of directors meeting in August 2015 that there was only $16,000 left on the mortgage, which was glad news. The finish line was in sight. They had no way to know at the time how crucial it would be to have that mortgage paid off by 2020. They carried on, blissfully unaware (like everyone else) of what was to come.

WomanKraft Gallery Opening Reception, June-July Show, June 3, 2017

Kat Cronn and Barbara Achord filled the positions of Membership Coordinator and Social Media Promotion. Geno Davis began updating the website. Mary Lou Griggs took over the Castle Voice newsletter, and Tony DiAngelo took on grounds maintenance. Momentum was strong.

In a sad turn of events, founding mother Carol Kestler passed away on July 17, 2015. Carol was a much loved Tucson treasure. A great supporter of the community and founder of Arts Genesis, Kestler was also an internationally recognized Judaica artist, jeweler, and a cherished friend of WomanKraft.

Another passing of note is that of longtime friend of WomanKraft, Wyatt Anthony, in 2018. The Arizona Historical Society accepted her portfolio, seeking to balance their collection with more female vision. She is greatly missed.

The building turned 100 years old in 2018; WomanKraft had been there for 26 years. The funny thing was, even though her women may have been showing signs of the passing of the years, the house herself seemed to be getting younger. The mortgage was fully paid off that year, and as the nonprofit turned 44 years old, WomanKraft finally had full equity in its own Castle.

Esperanza Dance Project
Photo Credit Skreko

Grace Rhyne left her position as executive director in 2018. In 2019 she returned with a fundraiser for the Esperanza Dance Project, a local nonprofit that speaks to children and young adults about surviving sexual violence. Esperanza performs in high schools where they provide information and resources, and talk with people afterwards. Her sister Zoe recalls the performance:

"Grace invited five emerging choreographers, and they each created a dance for a different part of the Castle. One person made a dance for the stage in the main building, another for the porch, and one for the classroom; there was someone upstairs, and someone dancing outside. We split the audience into groups, and they went on a tour. One group would see the dance in the main room and then they would go upstairs.

"Each group got to do their dance five times for five audiences. It was intimate and beautiful, and a lot like an art show; seeing the way the dancers interpreted the space was amazing. It must have been gratifying for the performers, because normally you work up to it and then you get to do it once, or maybe twice. It was such an interesting way of using the space and interacting with the community."

By 2019 the School of the Arts had expanded to 12 instructors and added 11 bilingual classes. Josh Smith and David Silvestri finished repairing exterior termite damage and repainted the outside of the building. Memberships, donations and art sales were up. Things were looking good as the decade wound down, and it appeared that exciting times were in store for 2020. Little did they know then how right they would be about that, and how much they would come to wish they hadn't been.

CHAPTER 13

UNRESTRAINED SPIRIT, 2020-2024

"The pandemic was really fucking terrible," says Zoe Rhyne. "Art is an impulse buy and everything is about audience. The hardest thing is getting people through the door, and once that was removed from our option it was awful. WomanKraft is an intimate space and the classroom is small, so there's usually a maximum of four or five people already. When we came back we had to go down to two, which meant we were paying teachers more than we were making from the students taking the classes, and that's not even considering supplies.

"Getting the audience back was also hard because we tended to serve an older demographic and they were the most susceptible, so they had every reason to be careful. Some people were very eager to get back out, and others were like *I may never come out of my house again.* We posted a couple of classes online, but that was hit or miss because it's difficult to make sure everybody has the same supplies when you're not there. So COVID stopped us in our tracks there for a minute. But I will say that when we finally did come back, a lot of people had been making art during the pandemic, so there was a lot to be seen."

Womankraft was one of the lucky ones, a small nonprofit that was able to drop anchor and sit it out. Because the mortgage had been paid off, and through the generosity of donors, the art center persevered.

The gallery and school went into crisis mode in 2020, scaling back where they could and shutting down what they couldn't. Receptions and other evening activities were cancelled. For the first time, the *Holiday Bizarre* and the rummage fairs were out. Class sizes were limited, masks required, and gallery hours reduced. Bingo Night in March was the last evening activity of the year, and afterward, the halls of the Castle rang with quiet.

Josh Smith set up an outdoor plant shop called Plantney (named after Britney Spears). Work continued on social media presence. Otherwise, WomanKraft, like most of the rest of the world, had nothing much else to do about the pandemic but wait.

Little by little, the lights came back on. The limit on class size was lifted after a year, in January 2021, and the gallery resumed regular hours. The School of the Arts began adding new classes. There was a vigorous clothing, blanket and food drive around the holidays. Things were starting to feel like normal again - sort of.

Receptions resumed in 2022; there was only one per show instead of two, but that was okay. It was just good to be having openings again. Class sizes increased and the School of the Arts added four new instructors. The *Wise Women Writing* Workshop resumed and the rummage fair recommenced.

There were some other organizational changes as the art center came back to life. Zoe Rhyne resigned as gallery director for personal reasons. Josh Smith left to start his own business. Geno Davis developed a virtual tour for the website and Nicole Young moved her business, Her Ladyship's Bazaar, into Studio #102. Nicole and Mary Lou Griggs joined the board of directors.

WomanKraft reported financial solvency at the annual 2023 board meeting; however, revenue from the School of the Arts was down due to the pandemic. In an attempt to attract new students the school began offering a 50% discount to Tucson teachers.

WomanKraft clambered back to its feet in 2023, with the gallery and the School of the Arts gaining traction once again. There were also two other significant accomplishments that year: one was the scrapbook project, funded by Nancy Martin and implemented by Caroline Latron, who corralled 45 years of flyers, playbills, and newsletters in no particular order into a cogent series of albums. That effort was the precursor to this book, which never could have been written without it.

Another worthy accomplishment was the book nook set up by Gerrie Young. She dug into the boxes languishing upstairs and put together an impressive library. At the front of the Castle is a small room with a few items for sale, and a wall full of shelves crammed with books that are mostly about art.

"People should come down and look at these," says Young. "We have a good selection and the prices are great."

One of the most exciting events of 2023, at least for many of the workers, was the addition of a smartphone which gave them wifi access and the ability to accept credit/debit cards.

WomanKraft faces some challenges in 2024. Filling executive level positions is one. Attracting volunteers in a tough economic climate is another. Gail Paul speaks to that: "I think we are in for some tough times ahead, politically and culturally, in this country. Then young people will find they need a center of support from places like WomanKraft, and the only way to get that is to volunteer. I think the times when we build our best community are when we feel it's threatened."

WomanKraft is bigger than any building: it's the unrestrained spirit of the founding mothers, the love of the community for art, and the passion of the artists who've made it happen for the past 50 years. Along the way, the organization has stayed true to its original vision: community based art and worker empowerment. Extraordinary possibilities lie ahead for the WomanKraft community, where people speak to each other in the language of art.

Photo Credit: Barbara Cooper

JUDY JENNINGS

Photo by Barbara Cooper

Judy Jennings spent her first night in Arizona in 1980, camping at the base of Pichacho Peak, where she was unexpectedly introduced to jumping cholla and javelina. The next day she discovered Fourth Avenue, Antigone Books, and the laid back vibe of Tucson; with that, the midwesterner was hooked. She made a mental note to show the desert a little more respect going forward, and got settled in.

Her stories about animal conservation have been published in *Wildlife Conservation Magazine*, *Bark Magazine* and the *Tucson Weekly*. Writing about the preservation of community-based arts has turned out to be similar in ways she hadn't considered before.

Judy is no stranger to day jobs, either; she's worked as a chef, taxicab driver, natural foods retailer, and wine retailer. These days, she volunteers with a dog rescue organization and enjoys writing creative nonfiction. She cut her teeth on the feminist movement of the 1970s, and still believes sisterhood is powerful. Dancing Traveler Tarot is Judy's other hat; she leads Tarot workshops and offers readings.

Possibly the most important thing for you to know about her is that she's very kind to animals, and most days her superpower is gratitude.

Contact info:

jjprairiedog@gmail.com

Dancingtravelertarot@instagram

Facebook: Judy Jennings

NANCY MARTIN

"Whatever concerns me has a way of coming through my work. I made my first clay mask in 1967, and the image and the material still seem to convey my meaning. I like the way the clay process, the nature of the material, and my image have come together."

N. Skreko Martin

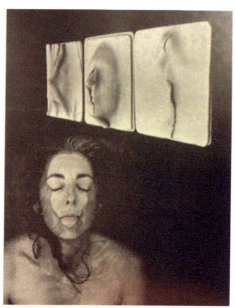

'Emergence Triptych' Dimension Porcelain
'WomanKraft at Pima' Workshops and Exposition, September 1977
N. Skreko Martin

Nancy Martin, known professionally as N. Skreko Martin, is one of six Tucson women artists who founded WomanKraft in 1974. Since moving to Tucson in 1971, Nancy has been a passionate advocate of community-based arts. Other nonprofit arts organizations she has worked with include Arts Genesis and the Arts and Media Task Force of the Tucson Women's Commission, where she was co-chair in 1976.

She was State Co-chair, Arizona Caucus for Women in the Arts in 1978, and Project Director and Grants Administrator for the CETA-funded Community Artists Project from 1979-1984. As Project Director for the Tucson Women's Cable Consortium Community Service Project Nancy secured funding in grants from community sources.

Her involvement with WomanKraft has included the position of Chief Grant Writer since inception, and she's served as Secretary for the board of directors since 1997. She has worked as Gallery Director with the Berta Wright, Impressions 11, and Beth O'Donnell galleries. An art educator and writer as well as a working artist, Nancy has taught through the Tucson Museum of Art, Pima College and University of Arizona continuing education, and WomanKraft.

Skreko Martin's commissions and awards are many, but one installation that's especially near and dear to her heart is the ceramic tile mural created in Tucson with a group of school children. *The Children's Mural*, a massive installation celebrating the children's contribution to the Pio Decimo Angel Children's Center, was created in 1982 and consists of ceramic tiles made from drawings by the children.

Over the course of her career Nancy has taught English in the public schools for seven years, spent one year as an art center director, 10 years as an organizer in the Tucson arts community, and 38 years as a working artist.

Skreko Martin's work has been exhibited in galleries from coast to coast in the United States, including the Renwick Gallery of the Smithsonian, the Hands of Man Gallery in New York, and the Woman's Art Center in San Francisco. She is included in the permanent collections of the Tucson Museum of Art, the Lakeview Center for the Arts and Sciences in Peoria, Illinois, and Bradley University. Corporate commissions and collections include the Hilton and Radisson Hotels, J D Searle Corporation, First National Bank of Tucson, Canyon Ranch, Peat Marwick and the Shorr Group in Chicago. Her work has been shown at the Phoenix Art Museum, the WomanKraft Gallery in Tucson, the University of Arizona, and Pima Community College.

N. Skreko Martin is an internationally recognized sculptor, as well, with several installations in Japan. In 1989 she received the Ueno Royal Museum Award in the 6th Henry Moore Grand Prize Exhibition at the Utsukushi-ga-hara Open Air Museum, where POWERGATE was placed in the permanent collection. Another commission, STARGATE, was installed at Queen's Square, Yokohama, Japan, a live/work/transportation/cultural complex.

Born in Chicago in 1939, Nancy's professional background includes study at the Art Institute of Chicago as a scholarship student 1950-1955, study in sculpture at the University of Hartford under Wolfgang Biehl, and a Master's degree from Bradley University in 1968. Additional study during that period included ceramics with James Hanson, sculpture with Nita Sunderland, and workshops with Peter Voulkos, Paul Soldner, Stan Vanderbeek and Allan Kaprow. She studied with Judy Chicago and the core faculty of the Feminist Studio Workshop in Los Angeles in 1976.

In 1977 Nancy toured Japan with emphasis on museums, temples, and gardens. This impactful trip offered her the opportunity to meet with Living National Treasures, Serizawa and Hamada.

Nancy also created several large-scale outdoor works. Her last one was AGRICULTURAL 111, a 500' x 600' mowing completed as an artists-in-residence for the Field Project in Oregon, Illinois.

Presently, Nancy is the only remaining WomanKraft founding mother still involved with the arts center (as of 2024), and she is the driving force behind the preservation of the group's history. Those of us who have worked with her along the way consider her to be our own Living Treasure.

Landscape R' 86x34x4" Polychromed Ceramic

GAYLE SWANBECK

'Rabbits' painted with coffee, detailed with India ink.
Gayle Swanbeck

Gayle doesn't remember a time when she wanted to be anything other than an artist. Born in 1950 in the small mining town of Ironwood, Michigan, she was dreaming of having her own gallery by the time she was in high school. Gayle studied at Michigan State University, where she received her Bachelor's in Fine Arts before moving to Tucson in 1970.

Once settled in the Old Pueblo, Gayle became well acquainted with the arts and crafts fair circuit. In1978 she joined the Community Artists Project, operating under the auspice of WomanKraft, where she became widely recognized for her skill as an art instructor and mentor, as well for her talent as a working artist. She taught classes at numerous senior housing facilities and community centers, including Tucson House where she established the annual *Young at Art* exhibition that continued through the WomanKraft Gallery for many years after the Community Artist Project ended.

Swanbeck served as adjunct faculty in the Senior Education program at Pima Community College 1984-2000. She became WomanKraft Director of Exhibits when the gallery on Congress Street opened in 1986, and has remained in that position to date (2024).

Gayle and Linn Lane, partners in both life and in WomanKraft, were together for 34 years, until Linn's passing in 2012.

LINN LANE, BELOVED GEMINI

June 1, 1947-October 6, 2012

Womankraft Member, Playwright, and Contributing Artist Since 1975

Womankraft Executive Director 1986-2012

"Women have traditionally told stories, engaged in group activities, kept journals and written letters ... As women we have found that sharing clarifies our thoughts".

Linn Lane

'WomanKraft at Pima' Workshops and Expositions, September, 1977

Linn Lane; poet, playwright, and intuitive passed peacefully after an eight year battle with Crohn's disease. She was survived by Gayle Swanbeck, her life partner of 33 years, her brother Wayne (Marty) Lane, her nieces and nephews Carrie (Eddie) Little, Landon (Dawn) Tate, Brady (Krista) Lane, and eight great nieces and nephews. She also left behind scores of dear friends and admirers of her work.

Linn was predeceased by her parents, A.D. and Fern Lila Knight Lane. Born in the "one-horse town" of Bayfield, Colorado, Linn went on to graduate from Farmington, New Mexico High School, and earned a Bachelor of Arts degree from the University of New Mexico.

She was such a precocious child that Linn's mother taught her to read before she started the first grade. Fern was the source of much creative inspiration for her daughter. Linn was born within one day of her mother's birthday, and died within one day of the day of her death.

A diary begun at the age of nine was Linn's first book. After settling in Tucson in 1974, she became an activist for the arts. The WomanKraft Arts Center at 388 South Stone Street is her legacy, along with scores of of original plays, stories and poems. Linn joined WomanKraft in its early days and assumed the role of executive director in 1986, remaining in that position until she passed. She founded the WomanKraft Mixed Media Players, WomanKraft Developmental Theater, WomanKraft Press and Anubis's Hideaway retail shop inside the Castle.

Linn was a prolific and provocative writer with a contagious passion for the written and spoken word. Her plays were produced at The WomanKraft gallery on Congress Street and other venues, often with Gayle Swanbeck directing. She also produced two film documentaries, two feature length films, one short film and two radio plays. Her three books were published through WomanKraft Press.

Linn Lane may have been elfin in stature, standing only 4'11" and weighing a mere 110 pounds, but she walked this earth as a Goddess - worshipping Amazon. Renowned as a Tarot card reader, interpreter of astrological charts and acclaimed for her scripted rituals, Linn also enjoyed teaching classes on Tarot and Dream Interpretation through WomanKraft.

Her cherished Gayle found these words scribbled on a sticky note in Linn's handwriting a few days after she passed:

GRAVE MARKER

"I've done this and I've done that

But all I've ever really cared to do again and again

Was to write a good poem and to write a good play

And journey through life with my beloved Gayle friend."

Linn Lane

SUSAN CHAMBERS

1944-1999

"Only the process. Designing, cutting, printing, drying.
Cleaning. Satisfaction. Joy.
Does there need to be more?"

Susan Chambers

Susan Chambers, 'WomanKraft at Pima' Workshops and Ehibition, 1977

Susan "Susie" Chambers, WomanKraft co-founder, passed away peacefully but far too soon on June 18, 1999, at the age of 55. She died of complications from surgery after battling a lung infection for five weeks. She left behind her brother Wid, husband Art McGregor, and an arts community that had prospered greatly under her influence.

Until she passed, Susan served as president of the WomanKraft Board of Directors, was active on the Tucson/Pima Arts Council, volunteered with Mobile Meals and supported numerous Tucson writers, musicians, and local charities. Arts Genesis received ongoing support through sales of cards featuring her watercolors; she was also famous for her samples of Japanese cooking at fundraising dinners for the Tucson Museum of Art. Carol Kestler of Arts Genesis wrote that Susan approached these efforts "with the finesse, sparkle, wit, wisdom and generosity that were Susie's trademark."

Susan was involved with Womankraft throughout her life as a contributing artist, organizer, and supporter. It was she who donated the $10,000 downpayment that made it possible for WomanKraft to purchase the building on Stone Avenue.

Tucson was Susan's home for 44 years, interspersed with extensive trips to her second home, Japan. Her love affair with that country began as a high school student when she traveled there with her classmate Margaret and Margaret's grandmother, Margaret Sanger. She returned later as part of the Experiment in International Living; a student exchange group affiliated with Sargent Shriver as sort of a precursor to the Peace Corps. It was on this trip that she met her "Japanese family" in Kobe, with whom she remained in close contact throughout the test of her life.

She went on to gain her Bachelor of Arts degree from the University of Arizona. "I don't remember her major at the U of A," says her brother Wid, "only that she had the highest grade point average in the entire school every year she attended, out of, what, eight trillion students? Seems impossible, but that was Susie for you."

Susan took her Master's Degree in Japanese Language at Stanford. Wid remembers they both took a class there from the legendary design teacher Matt Kahn. "He was pretty much the reason she decided to switch it up and become an artist," says Wid. "He inspired a lot of students, everyone wanted to take his classes. *Introduction to Design* was possibly the best art class ever."

Susan was inspired to begin working with textiles and entered into her most exciting learning period when she apprenticed for a year in Tokyo with Serizawa, the renowned stencil dryer and Living Cultural Treasure. In time, Susan also took up painting, but fabric embellishment always remained her first love.

Susan and her mother, Freda Macadam Chambers, presented a joint exhibit at the WomanKraft Gallery in 1995. She and her husband, Art McGregor, had another in October, 1999, but sadly Susan passed in June and that became a memorial show.

Among places her work has been exhibited are the Scottsdale Center for the Arts, the Tubac Art Association, the Tucson Museum of Art, Pima Community College, the University of Arizona, Sky Harbor International Airport and the WomanKraft Gallery.

EACH ARTIST WAS ASKED THESE QUESTIONS:

How did you become involved?

What's your role?

What performance or exhibit have you found to be the most memorable?

What do you think is the key to WomanKraft's longevity?

What is WomanKraft's greatest accomplishment?

What's her greatest challenge?

How did the pandemic affect WomanKraft?

Where do you see the organization five years from now?

APPENDIX 2:
THE DANCERS OF ESPERANZA DANCE TROUPE

(Listed Alphabetically by First Name)

Beth Braun, Founder and Managing Artistic Director

Aaron Sorensen

Anna Campbell

Ariel Helm

Cassidy Saunders

Elizabeth Le

Emily Davis

Gabi West

Grace Rhyne

Janis Lee

Jaynie Anguiano

Megan Sorensen

Porfirio (Rio) Leon

Samantha Transue

Tadeo Valdez-Celaya

Veronica Pasamante

Zoe Falco

ACKNOWLEDGEMENTS

The Lioness share of credit for this account goes to Nancy Martin, who understood the importance of having a record of WomanKraft herstory, and reached out to make it happen. She has collaborated on every chapter, as well as secured funding for publication.

Credit goes to Gayle Swanbeck as well, for her storytelling largess and her patience with the process.

Finally, a huge shout out to everyone who took the time to respond to my queries and tell me your stories, thank you.

'Powergate' in Japan
N. Skreko Martin